Winning Poker Strategies

Crush Your Opponents and Master the Game

Table of Contents

Chapter 1. Introduction

Unleash the fearsome card shark within you and conquer your opponents with our Special Report on "Winning Poker Strategies: Crush Your Opponents and Master the Game". This meticulously crafted guide is a treasure chest filled to the brim with coveted tips and strategies, taking you on a riveting journey from the basic bluffing techniques right up to the intricate bluff-detection methods employed by seasoned poker pros. Whether you're a beginner still fumbling with your chips or an old hand seeking to refine your game, we promise that with this report in your arsenal, you'll gain the confidence and skills to turn every bet into a win, every face into a poker face, and every game into an adrenaline-pumping brawl. Get ready to mesmerize, dominate, and stack up those chips with a victorious grin!

Chapter 2. Understanding the Basics: A Deep Dive into Poker's Essentials

Poker is an intriguing combination of probability, psychology, and strategy. It's a game where mastering the basics is absolutely essential, leading to enhanced skill development and the confidence to stake higher bets. We'll start our deep dive into poker's essentials with the basic rules and objectives of the game before delving into poker hand rankings, betting structures, and betting styles.

2.1. Rules and Objectives: The Heart of the Game

Poker is played with a standard 52-card deck, and the objective is to win your opponents' chips. This can be accomplished in two ways: making the best five-card hand at the end of a round, or convincing your opponents to fold through strategic betting, even if your hand isn't necessarily the best.

During a poker round, cards are dealt to each player, and rounds of betting take place where players can bet, call, raise, or fold based on the strength they perceive their hand to have. The player who stays in the game until the end and has the best hand (or the last remaining player after the others have folded) wins all the chips in the pot.

2.2. Poker Hand Rankings: Know Your Strength

Comprehending hand rankings is fundamental to understanding

poker. From highest to lowest, the rankings are as follows:

1. Royal Flush: A-K-Q-J-10 of the same suit

2. Straight Flush: Five consecutive cards of the same suit

3. Four of a kind: Four cards of the same rank

4. Full House: Three of a kind and a pair

5. Flush: Five cards of the same suit, not sequential

6. Straight: Five consecutive cards of different suits

7. Three of a kind: Three cards of the same rank

8. Two pair: Two different pairs

9. One pair: Two cards of the same rank

10. High card: The highest card when no other hand applies

It's important to memorize these rankings as it's fundamental to your decision-making process during the game.

2.3. Betting Structures: Structured, Pot Limit, No Limit

Poker can be played with various betting structures, generally falling into the categories of Structured (Limit), Pot Limit, or No Limit.

In Structured Limit poker, bets and raises are of a fixed amount. For Pot Limit games, players can bet or raise up to the current total pot. Lastly, in No Limit poker, players can bet all their chips at any time.

Each structure brings its own element of strategy. For instance, No Limit games often lead to larger pots and drastic swings in chip stacks due to the unrestricted betting.

2.4. Betting Actions: Bet, Check, Call, Raise, Fold

Understanding each betting action is critical as it forms the strategic pulse of the game. Initially, you will have the option to Bet or Check. Betting involves placing a wager, while Checking is used to abstain from betting, passing the action to the next player.

Should a player Bet, the next player has the option to Call (match the bet), Raise (increase the bet), or Fold (surrender the hand, losing any existing chips in the pot).

Remember, betting is not just about money. It's a way to communicate. By observing your opponents' betting actions, you can gain insights into their potential hand strengths and gameplay tendencies.

2.5. The Art of Bluffing: Foxing your Foes

Bluffing is a vital aspect of poker where a player bets or raises with a weak hand to lead opponents into believing he/she has a stronger hand, thus inducing them to fold. Bluffing is a powerful tool that increases unpredictability and can help you win regardless of the cards in your hand.

However, it's a double-edged sword. A failed bluff can lead to significant losses. The art lies not in bluffing frequently but in choosing the right moment to bluff. This is largely dictated by your position, the number of players left, and their playing styles.

2.6. Poker Positions: Early, Middle, Late

Your position in a poker game refers to where you sit in relation to the dealer. The player to the left of the dealer is in the Early Position, and is required to bet first, while players at the other end are in the Late Position, providing them the advantage of observing others play before they make their move.

In addition, the Middle Position players are sandwiched between these two points. Strategic decisions and the effectiveness of bluffs can be significantly influenced by your position.

Poker boasts a rich strategic landscape, and it rewards those who continually learn and adapt. In the next chapter, we delve deeper into gameplay strategies, exploring how various factors, from player psychology to table dynamics, can be leveraged to improve your win rate. But, by understanding and mastering these poker basics, you've slid your first vital chips into the pot.

Chapter 3. Mastering Poker Etiquette: Refine Your Table Manners

Mastering table etiquette is more than just knowing when to hold or fold; it's understanding the unwritten rules of poker that foster a respectful, enjoyable game for all.

3.1. Handling Poker Chips

One of the first principles of poker etiquette revolves around the handling of poker chips. Accurate chip stacking and management not only makes it easier for you and your opponents to keep track of the game state, but also demonstrates professionalism and consideration toward other players and game officials.

1. Always keep your chips clearly visible and accurately stacked.

2. Don't throw, splash or toss your chips into the pot.

3. Refrain from handling other players' chips without their permission.

3.2. Betting Etiquette

Observing betting etiquette ensures smooth gameplay, prevents unintentional signals or 'tells', and maintains the game's integrity. Gathering betting etiquette wisdom includes understanding when and how you should make a bet, and being respectful of the betting process of others.

1. Make sure your actions are clear and brisk. Vague or slow actions can disrupt the game flow.

2. State your intentions before you move your chips. This reduces confusion and maintains game flow.

3. Refrain from string betting. Declare your total bet upfront, or push all your chips at once.

4. Respect the "one player to a hand" rule. Avoid giving or asking for advice during a game.

3.3. Maintaining Poker Table Decorum

Staying respectful and patient ensures a friendly atmosphere around the poker table. No matter how intense the game gets, maintaining your composure and thoughtfulness toward others is an unspoken requirement.

1. Refrain from criticizing other people's play. Treat all players with respect regardless of skill level.

2. Keep your emotions in check. Don't let a bad beat or a streak of bad luck negatively affect your behavior.

3. Avoid excessive celebration when you win a hand. Be respectful toward players who just lost.

3.4. Language and Conversation at the Poker Table

Language is a powerful tool that can misshape perceptions and cause unnecessary controversy if used incorrectly. The poker table demands a careful use of words.

1. Do not discuss a hand while it's still ongoing. Talking about a hand in progress could influence gameplay.

2. Use respectful language at all times. Avoid profanities and

offensive comments.

3. Keep conversations light and non-provocative. Refrain from discussing sensitive topics.

3.5. Managing Downtime

During downtime, it's important to remember that, even though you're not actively playing, you're still at the table.

1. Use your phone, eat, or read a book only if it does not disrupt the game pace or concentration of other players.

2. Pay attention to the play, even when you're not involved in a hand.

3.6. Handling Winning and Losing

Poker's true nature is a game of skill and chance combined. All players will have their fair share of wins and losses.

1. Show grace in defeat and celebration in victory, always demonstrating good sportsmanship.

2. Congratulate winners genuinely, even if you're the one they just defeated.

3. Maintaining an even temperament despite a big win or loss is the mark of a truly refined poker player.

Being cognizant and respectful of these etiquette rules will not only make you a player that others enjoy competing with, but also positively influence the way you handle the psychology of the game. When paired with a sound understanding of strategy and skill, mastering the etiquette of poker will translate to a class of gameplay that will consistently bring you a step closer to victory.

Chapter 4. Striking with Strategy: Tactical Approaches to Every Hand

Poker is a game of strategy, a complex confluence of risk, reward, and uncertainty. The mathematics of the game is crucial, but what separates the good from the great is a profound understanding of strategic play. It combines an awareness of position, a knack for discernment in body language, and an inherent ability to play the mental game. As such, this discussion revolves around an array of tactical approaches that can be used in different situations, whether you're playing online, at a home game, or in a high-stakes tournament at the Bellagio.

4.1. Positional Play: Using 'The Button' to Your Advantage

On the poker table, where you sit matters. The dealer button gives you the privilege of being the last to act, allowing you to observe your opponent's actions before you make your decision. This positional advantage cannot be overstated. An optimal strategy is to play tight from early positions and broaden your range significantly when you are on or close to the button.

4.2. Playing Styles and Your Strategic Approach

There are four main types of poker players: tight-passive, tight-aggressive, loose-passive, and loose-aggressive. Knowing how to identify these player types early and adjusting your play accordingly is vital.

Tight-passive players fold often and play few hands. They're risk-averse and mostly stay in the hand if they have strong cards. Against them, increase your aggression.

Tight-aggressive players also play fewer hands, but they're not afraid to bet or raise when they do. Patience is key against these opponents since they often let the weak hands go.

Loose-passive players see a lot of flops and play a wide range of hands, making them easy to bluff. Against them, tighten your game and pounce when you have strong cards.

Loose-aggressive players play many hands, often betting and raising. Against them, tighten your game and do not take unnecessary risks. Let them make mistakes which you can capitalize on.

4.3. The Art of the Bluff

Bluffing is an indispensable tool in the poker player's arsenal. Yet, a bluff is not merely lying about the strength of your hand. It's about telling a convincing story that dissuades your opponent from challenging you.

Successful bluffing often has more to do with 'how' and 'when' than with 'what'. It's about seizing the right opportunities. Be observant, assess the texture of the flop, your opponent's betting patterns, and their likely hand ranges. Remember, an ill-timed bluff can be catastrophic.

4.4. Using Probability and Hand Reading

Poker is, at its heart, a game of percentages. Learn the odds for common situations, like the likelihood of hitting a flush draw on the turn or the river, to support your decision-making process.

Hand reading is the complex art of deducing an opponent's likely range of hands based on clues they've provided: their playing style, position, bet-sizing, and overall table image. Remember, it's about ranges, not specific hands. It helps to ask yourself what hands they would play in the same manner.

4.5. The Power of Bet Sizing

Bet sizing is a subtle yet potent weapon. A larger bet usually signals strong hands, while a smaller bet implies weaker hands or an attempt to induce your action. Adjust your bet sizes based on what you want to achieve - to call or fold - and don't fall into patterns that can be easily identified. Your bets should be uncorrelated with your hand strength to maintain ambiguity and deny your opponent any reading advantage.

4.6. Understanding Implied Odds

Implied odds refer to the additional money you expect to win if you hit your hand. Knowing to use implied odds can help when facing difficult decisions with drawing hands. Formulate your bets considering potential future earnings, which could negate any immediate pot odds discrepancy.

4.7. Practicing Emotional Control

Poker is a game that can stir intense emotion. Emotional control is one of the most critical aspects of poker that has nothing to do with cards. Never let your emotions dictate your plays; instead, make decisions based on rationality and strategic consideration.

If you follow the outlined strategies, you'll navigate the poker landscape more astutely. Nevertheless, remember that poker is a lifelong learning process. Embrace the continuous growth journey and may you always have an ace up your sleeve!

Chapter 5. Hold 'Em High: Dominating Texas Hold'em

In the realm of modern poker, Texas Hold'em stands as the most widely played variant – a king uncontested on its glimmering throne. This game, bathed in glory and braced with the sheer dynamics of human calculation and randomness, waits to be tamed by those willing to learn, adapt, and master its fascinating nuances. This guide is designed to provide comprehensive insights into understanding and dominating this complex game of strategy, observation, and well-informed risk-taking.

Texas Hold'em – often simply referred to as 'Hold'em' – is both intricate and exciting. A combination of community and hole cards, it's the pivot around which the entire skill set of poker revolves. Being proficient in Hold'em implies a strength in your overall poker abilities.

5.1. Knowing the Basics

Before delving into complex strategies and maneuvers, one must have a clear understanding of the basic principles guiding Texas Hold'em. Each player is dealt two private cards, known as 'hole cards'. Five community cards are dealt face-up on the 'board'. All players in the game use their two hole cards in combination with the five community cards to each pursue the best possible five-card poker hand. The player with the highest ranking hand at showdown wins the pot.

The structure of betting in Hold'em can be in any format - limit, no limit, or pot limit game formats primarily. It seems simple, doesn't it? But don't be fooled by the seeming simplicity of the game, for the complexity lies in the strategies and mind games employed during play.

5.2. Pre-Flop Strategies

The pre-flop stage of a game, where players are dealt their hole cards, is the first instance where strategy comes into play. An excellent pre-flop strategy begins by considering the strength of your hole cards. Higher cards and pairs tend to be stronger, but the position at the table significantly influences this as well.

Early position players are at a disadvantage as they have to act without knowing what the other players plan to do. Therefore, you should play only strong hands in these positions, such as high pairs (Queens, Kings, Aces) or high Suited connectors like Ace-King.

In a **middle position**, you can afford to play a wider range of hands. Lower pairs and suitable connectors can be played, taking into account the actions of those in early positions.

As a **late position** player who is one of the last to act, you have the most information at your disposal. You can widely expand your range of playable hands, adapting and fluctuating your gameplay based on earlier player's actions.

However, these are not rigid rules. They provide a guideline, and the key is to adapt your strategy based on your observations of other player's behaviors, their perceived hand strength, and your ambition to win.

5.3. The Art of Bluffing

A crucial aspect of the game, bluffing, could be considered an art unto itself. Successfully bluffing involves making your opponents believe you have a better hand than you actually possess. This implied strength can force other players to fold their hands, awarding you the pot.

Significantly, a good bluff is not just about holding a poor hand and displaying confidence. It also includes pretending to have a weaker hand when you have a strong one, prompting opponents to keep betting and swelling the pot – a maneuver known as 'slow playing'.

However, bluff judiciously. Seasoned players can detect persistent bluffers and might call your bluff at the wrong time for you. So save your bluffs for the right moment and against the right players.

5.4. Reading Your Opponents

Becoming adept at reading your opponents and deciphering their poker tells is a skill that separates the novices from the veterans. Tells can be anything from subtle facial expressions to how someone places a bet or handles their chips. Mastering this ability to 'read' other players adds a potent layer to your game.

Physical tells, while often depicted in pop culture, are less common in real-life games but can still provide valuable information about a player's hand. People who try to appear unusually relaxed may be bluffing, while those who suddenly stiffen up might have a strong hand. Similarly, behavioral tells like how hurriedly a bet is placed or if there's hesitancy can also give away a lot.

Online games, where physical tells are unavailable, require a different kind of observation. Look out for betting patterns among your opponents – Do they raise or fold under certain circumstances consistently? Do they take more time to make a decision when they are weak? Are they trying to intimidate others into folding by betting aggressively despite weak hands (also called 'Bullying')? Conscious current recognition of these patterns can be instrumental in predicting an opponent's actions.

5.5. Post-Flop Strategies - The Turn & River

After the pre-flop betting round, dealing with the 'flop,' 'turn,' and 'river' - the community cards - constitutes the post-flop play. Each of these stages requires their specific strategies.

The Flop: After viewing the first three community cards, players have a better understanding of the potential value of their hand. Here strategy involves an evaluation of whether the flop has enhanced your hand (by, say, completing a pair or a flush), whether you can draw valuable combinations in future rounds, and the likeliness of your opponents holding a better hand than yours. It's essential to consider these aspects before proceeding with your betting strategy.

The Turn: The 'turn' card can significantly change players' perceived hand strength. When the fourth community card provides advantage, be prepared to play aggressively to protect that hand. Conversely, if your hand seems weak after the turn, it's advisable to fold unless the size of the pot justifies a call or if you think you can successfully bluff your way through.

The River: The 'river' card offers the final chance to improve your hand. Here, understanding how the card changes your hand relative to the potential hands your opponents might have is key. Be conservative if the river card isn't in your favor, but if it completes your hand, bet aggressively.

5.6. Managing Your Bankroll

While the art of bluffing, reading your opponents, and understanding post-flop tactics are crucial, they form part of a broader Winning Poker Strategy - managing your bankroll. It involves a set of rules about how much of your poker funds you should invest in a game to maximize profits and limit losses.

Finding a correct balance that matches your skill level, game type, and financial comfort zone can improve not only your winnings but also prolong your poker career. It's essential never to bet more than you can afford to lose, as unpredictability and variance are an integral part of the game.

5.7. Conclusion

Mastering Texas Hold'em poker demands dedication, time, and keen observation. It requires both rational mathematical strategy and an understanding of the more human elements of the game. As you absorb this know-how and evolve your gameplay, remember that rationale over emotion, discipline over recklessness, and patience over haste are the true hallmarks of a Texas Hold'em champion. By combining these qualities with the strategies mentioned herein, you're sure to surpass the competition and lead the poker boards!

Chapter 6. Bluffing Brilliance: Deception as an Art Form

Understanding the intrinsic art of bluffing becomes requisite when diving into the deep waters of a challenging card game like poker. This versatile tool, when wielded wisely, can become a potent weapon that brings even the mightiest opponents to their knees and swings the odds in your favor. When mismanaged, however, it could lead to swift and punishing retribution. The difference lies in knowing when, how, and whom to bluff.

6.1. Determining When to Bluff

Careful consideration of when to bluff might turn a basic trick into a powerful stratagem. Bluffing isn't a catch-all move, but a wisely appointed maneuver that must be deployed in response to the table's shape, your hand's quality, and your opponents' perceived weaknesses.

To start with, the size of the table can significantly influence your bluffing decisions. You should generally prefer to bluff at smaller tables, as there are fewer players to convince that you have a winning hand. Conversely, a bluff at a larger table requires that each player either folds or believes in the veracity of your feint, making bluffs riskier and more challenging.

In playing the game, you also need to assess your hand, and, more importantly, the hands that your opponents think you have. A well-timed bluff's success hinges significantly on your table image and how plausible your bluff is based on your previous plays. If you have been playing conservatively, getting aggressive with a weak hand could be interpreted as a strong hand, making your bluff more effective.

Finally, it is paramount to target the right person or people when you do bluff. Attempting to bluff a novice, who may not be a tactical enough player to fold even with a weak hand, could backfire horribly. Similarly, trying to bluff a seasoned player without a convincing set-up is akin to amateur poker suicide.

6.2. The Art of the Semi-Bluff

While demonstrations of bluffing brilliance typically involve someone brazenly pushing piles of chips into the pot with nothing more than a high card, it's the semi-bluff that often proves far more effective in the competitive realm of poker.

If the standard bluff is the 'smoke and mirrors' of poker, the semi-bluff is the 'cloak and dagger.' Rather than trying to convince everyone else at the table that a weak hand is strong, a semi-bluff involves making bets or raises with a hand that could potentially become strong. The semi-bluff is a win-win move in essence: if your opponents fold, you win the pot; if you draw the card you need, you might end up with the strongest hand.

6.3. Bet Sizing and Bluffing

The size of your bet is a vital tell in poker, a factor that could spell the doom or the victorious ring of a bluff. The adage 'bet enough to make them fold, but not more than you have to' can guide your bluff's size, but the true mastery of this aspect of bluffing stems from the understanding of your opponents.

Consider the psychology of the player across from you. If your opponent is the type to get stubborn at the sign of aggression, a major push may only agitate them into calling or raising even with a weaker hand. If they're skittish, just the smallest hint of strength in your wager might be enough to send them packing.

Bet sizing significantly comes into play when attempting to sell your semi-bluff believably. The effective semi-bluff should lure opponents into assuming you've got a strong hand, even if you're only holding onto a potential. Persuade them sufficiently, and they'll unwillingly yield the pot.

6.4. Spotting an Opponent's Bluff

Mastering the art of bluffing also involves being able to spot your opponents' bluffs. Investing time in understanding individual players is crucial in this aspect. For some players, bluffing might be a sporadic play while for others it might be a regular occurrence, a part of their gameplay.

Look for behaviors that diverge from their usual patterns. Changes could be subtle, like betting slightly more or less than they usually do, hesitating before making a move, or changing their conversational patterns.

Being observant of 'tells' is also crucial. A tell is a change in a player's behavior or demeanor that is thought to provide clues to that player's assessment of their hand. Some players might bluff when they're nervous, while others bluff only when they're excessively confident.

6.5. Harnessing Your Poker Face

A poker face is a facial expression devoid of any tell-tale signs that could potentially hint at the strength of your cards. Despite the natural instinct to react to different hands, maintaining a poker face keeps you secure from betraying any unintended information to your opponents.

While maintaining a poker face might seem as simple as keeping a straight face, it extends beyond that. It involves reigning control over your entire gestural spectrum: body language, eye movements, even the tone of your voice. All of these can be potential tells, and the masterful player learns to keep all under control whether they're sitting on a coveted royal flush or a lousy 2-7 offsuit.

Mastering the bluff and the counter-bluff, then, doesn't just mean controlling your actions—it means studying those of everyone else at the table. Bluffing is mind games, probability, and raw daring all rolled into one. It can break your opponents, shatter alliances, and flip the game on its head in a single moment. But remember, with each bluff, the stakes rise and bluffing should be used sparingly. Overbluffing might lead your opponents to read you like an open book. After all, poker's magical allure is its balance of luck, strategy, and the infinite mind games played around the green-felt battlefield.

Chapter 7. Reading Tells: Deciphering Hidden Messages in Gameplay

The ability to read tells, those subtle shifts in behavior, expressions, or patterns that signal a player's inner state or intentions, is a key skill that distinguishes an average player from a poker shark. By learning to decipher these hidden messages, you can understand your opponents better and make winning decisions. This chapter provides an in-depth exploration into the art of reading poker tells, guiding you towards raising your poker IQ effortlessly.

7.1. Body Language, Gestures, and Blink Rate

It's been said that communication is only 7% verbal and the rest is non-verbal. Thus, a keen eye on your opponents' body language is an essential part of your tell-reading regimen. It's like a silent dialogue which, if interpreted correctly, can reveal an opponent's hand without them uttering a single word.

Watch an opponent's shoulders. Are they tense, hunched or relaxed? Rapid movements or trembling hands are usually signs of nervousness which may indicate a weak hand. Gestures too, when inconsistent with normal behavior, often betray an insightful tell. An opponent who is overly demonstrative might be bluffing to cover a poor hand whereas someone conspicuously silent might be holding a strong hand.

Blink rate also deserves your attention. It's been observed that players often blink quicker when they are nervous or bluffing, and slower when they are confident and have a strong hand. But, remember, each player is different. What works with one might not work with another. Skillfully observe, catalog, and apply these tells to each player individually.

7.2. Analyzing Betting Patterns

Betting patterns are where the rubber hits the road in poker. They represent the most common and reliable tells, making them a crucial piece in the puzzle of decoding an opponent's strategy.

Consistently observe and mentally catalog your opponents' actions. How quickly do they bet when they have a strong hand? Do they consistently bluff on the river? By identifying an opponent's betting tendencies, you can anticipate their moves and strategize your responses accordingly. Remember, though, that experienced players may frequently change their betting patterns, making it important to stay adaptable and keep your observations up to date.

7.3. Facial Expressions and 'Poker Face'

Despite attempts to maintain a neutral 'poker face', facial expressions are potent divulgers of information. Micro-expressions, fleeting involuntary facial expressions that occur as fast as 1/15 to 1/25 of a second, are particularly revealing. While it's far from easy to detect these expressions, with practice, this becomes an incredibly powerful tool in your poker arsenal.

Do they have 'smiling eyes' or a forced smile when they bluff? Do they furrow their brow subconsciously when they have a strong hand? Every player will have their unique ticks, and spotting these can give you a significant edge.

7.4. Speech Patterns and Verbal Tells

An opponent's verbal interactions hold rich insights. Pay close attention to inconsistencies between their talk and their play. A player who advertises a strong hand verbally is more likely to be masking a weak one, while a player who downplays their hand probably holds strong cards.

Watch for changes in an opponent's speed of speech, tone, and content of their conversation. A sudden change could hint towards unease or excitement about their cards. Again, patterns are player-specific. Continuous observation and pattern recognition are key factors in successfully decoding verbal tells.

7.5. Psychological Tells and Player Profiling

Understanding the psychology of poker is about getting into your opponents' heads and anticipating their reactions. It goes beyond just spotting physical signs and engages you in a deeper analysis of a player's attitude, play style, and mindset.

Player profiling is about categorizing players based on their behavior and style of play. Recognizing player types, like tight-aggressive, loose-passive etc., can considerably aid in predicting their moves. Once you identify a player's type, you can tailor your strategy to take advantage of their inherent weaknesses.

7.6. Counteracting and Misdirecting Tells

Now that you have the tools to read tells, it's essential to ensure you aren't broadcasting your own. Maintain a consistent demeanor, regardless of your hand's strength. Vary your betting speeds occasionally to confound opponents. Evolve your playstyle to prevent getting profiled accurately.

Deception is as important as detection in poker. Misdirecting tells, where you deliberately project false tells, can equally unbalance your opponents, causing them to misread your hand and make costly mistakes.

Whether you're battling it out on the green felt of a classic casino, or testing your mettle in the dynamic world of online poker, understanding and interpreting tells gives you an unmatched edge. By focusing not just on the cards, but the players holding them, you can transcend from being a regular poker player to becoming a feared predator on the poker circuit. Like any valuable tool, mastering the art of reading tells demands patience and practice. Over time, these strategies will become second nature, elevating your game from poker enthusiast to seasoned pro. Remember, poker isn't a game of random luck, rather, it's a game of assessed risks. And mastering tells is a quantum leap towards measured risk-taking.

Chapter 8. Defending Against Bluffs: Techniques for Exposing Deception

Mastering poker is not just about perfecting your bluffing game, but becoming adept at detecting and neutralizing your opponent's deceptive strategies as well. As such, the principle focus of this chapter is to empower you to withstand bluffs, proficiently decipher your adversary's poker face, and act accordingly.

8.1. Know Your Opponents

Being able to read your opponents effectively is an essential skill in poker. While each player is unique in their strategy and demeanor, certain patterns usually emerge over time. Observing these patterns can provide key insights into their level of confidence, their present hand, and likelihood of them bluffing.

To start with, a player's betting pattern can be tremendously revealing. Most players heed the old advice, "Never bluff in a losing position," which generates a trend in their play style. Players tend to bluff more when they're winning, so recognize this and act accordingly.

Notice also each player's emotions and physiological responses. Increased heart rate, fidgeting, and nervous tics often indicate a bluff. Moreover, players often subconsciously mimic strength when weak and weakness when strong, so an overly intimidating demeanor could be a signal of void. Conversely, feigned meekness could imply a powerful hand.

Remember, it's all about observation and correlation. Aside from their behavior during various game situations, observe how they respond after revealing their hand. When you can correlate previous actions with actual hand strengths, you begin to build a working model of that player's behaviors.

8.2. Placing Pressure

People respond differently under pressure. Some rise to the challenge while others falter. A common tactic to expose a bluff is by placing your opponents under stress. This doesn't always mean placing a big bet or raising. You need to apply pressure in a way that makes your opponent uneasy about their bluff.

One way to apply pressure is "the probe bet". This is a smaller than normal bet intended to gather information. It is small enough to not risk too much but just enough to force a reaction. Monitoring how your opponents respond to these can give you valuable intel on their confidence level.

Another method is "the re-raise". If you suspect a bluff, a well-timed re-raise can put your opponent into a difficult decision, forcing them to either come clean, fold, or lie deeper.

8.3. Analyze Betting Patterns

Being perceptive to betting patterns is a crucial part of deciphering bluffs. Pay close attention to how your opponents bet when they have a strong hand, a weak hand, or when they're bluffing.

An abrupt change in betting style can be an obvious bluff indicator. If a typically conservative player suddenly makes a bold move, they may be bluffing. The reverse is also often true: when a typically loose-aggressive player suddenly becomes cautious their hand might be weaker than they want you to believe.

8.4. Master the Art of Hand Reading

Hand reading is a more advanced strategy, one that requires some knowledge of poker theory. The goal with hand reading is to assign your opponent a range of possible hands based on their actions and style of play.

To successfully read hands, a strong understanding of preflop play is vital. Know which hands people are likely to play from each position; for instance, a raise from an early position could indicate a much stronger hand than a raise from a late position.

Once you have a general idea about the range of hands your opponent might have, try to narrow down that range by interpreting their bets, reactions, and other behavior.

8.5. Protecting Yourself Against Reverse Bluffs

Good players may expect you to call their bluffs, and they prepare to counteract your defensive measures. This ploy is known as a 'reverse bluff', whereby an opponent pretends to bluff, provoking a reaction, but then revealing a strong hand. To counteract this, diversify your reactions to potential bluffs to stay unpredictable. Your ability to oscillate between passive and aggressive responses will help you hold your ground against the best of players.

A solid defense against bluffs is to be the player no one wants to bluff against. Stay unpredictable, diligent, and perceptive, and the bluffing battlefield will seem less daunting. Remember, the most victorious warriors win first and then go to war, while defeated warriors go to war first and then seek to win.

Chapter 9. Playing Your Position: Tailoring Strategy by Seat Placement

Understand the poker table as a battlefield, where each seat comes with its own set of advantages and perils. The seat you occupy during a poker hand can drastically influence your playing choices and overall game strategy. This chapter will arm you with the necessary strategies and expert tactics tailored to different seat positions.

9.1. The Early Positions

In a traditional nine-handed table, the early positions are the first three seats to the left of the big blind. Initially, these seats are considered challenging due to their lack of information on other players' hands.

After the first round of bets, or the pre-flop, the players in early positions have to make their decisions based on assumptions rather than substantial information. This is a tremendous disadvantage and must be accounted for in your strategy. The general recommendation for players in early positions is to play hands conservatively and firmly. Stick with strong hands, and fold weaker ones quickly with no remorse.

But playing conservatively doesn't mean you should become predictable. Mixing up your play with the occasional bluff or semi-bluff can give you an air of unpredictability, which is crucial in a game of poker. Nevertheless, exercise caution and determine when the situation is most advantageous to bluff while sitting in an early position.

9.2. Middle Positions

The middle positions are the three seats following the early positions. Being in a middle position provides a bit more flexibility than an early position.

From the middle positions, you can start to incorporate a wider range of hands into your play. That's because you'll see the moves of the early position players. You can harness this additional information to fine-tune your strategies, likely wager, and potential hands.

But as you make decisions, keep in mind that there are still players to act after you. Therefore, make your bets with enough conviction to challenge your immediate opponents, but also consider the unpredictability of the later players' actions. Walking this thin line and balancing your aggression is a masterful skill that can yield excellent dividends at the poker table.

9.3. Late Positions

The late positions comprise the last three seats, including the dealer, small blind, and big blind. These positions generally have the most information about what's happening in a hand because they act last pre-flop.

Playing in a late position allows you great flexibility in your play by providing you with the opportunity to observe your opponents' actions before your turn comes around. Hence, you can play a broader range of hands profitably. Your strategy from late positions can indeed be much more aggressive, liberal, and opportunistic compared to earlier positions.

However, don't forget that late positions also come with their set of challenges and risks. Your opponents would have gathered enough information about your playing style as the game progresses. Hence, switching tactics occasionally, diversifying your bet sizes, and introducing tactical semi-bluffs can be very beneficial when playing from these positions.

9.4. Positional Play and Table Dynamics

Understanding how table dynamics change with varying player positions is an essential part of a winning strategy. Being aware of who's left to act after you, how they've been playing, and what their stack size is are all crucial aspects that can affect your strategic decisions.

For instance, if the players to your left are playing tight, you can loosen up. Conversely, if they're playing loose, you might have to tighten up. This kind of adaptive positional strategy can help you grasp the subtle exploitative opportunities that arise during the game, allowing you to profit from them.

Remember, all these seat-based strategies should be in sync with your overall game plan, the type of opponents you're playing against, and the stage of the tournament you're at. As a thoughtful poker player, your goal is to consistently make decisions that maximize your expected value based on your position and all the available data points at your disposal.

Mastering positional play will undoubtedly require time and experience. But make no mistake, understanding the inherent power of position can turn you from being a mere player at the table to a fierce competitor who commands respect and fear in every seat you occupy.

Chapter 10. Risk and Reward: Navigating the Landscape of Betting

Understanding the dynamics of betting is the lifeblood of poker. A robust betting strategy not only keeps you afloat but dictates the course of the game. It drowns the bets of your opponents and sieves through their bluffs, making you the dominant force at the table. Betting is the primary source of initiating action in poker. It's a dangerous game of weaving through risks and rewards, and knowing it inside out is what separates the men from the boys.

10.1. The Art of Bet Sizing

Before we delve into the subtleties of bet sizing, it's crucial to understand its importance in the grand scheme of things. Bet sizing could dramatically influence the result of each round. The stakes you place, the timing, and the frequency - everything accumulates into forming an overall impression about your game style. Your opponents constantly analyze these patterns, just as you do theirs. Therefore, maintaining a balanced betting size becomes a pivotal part of your strategy.

The general rule of thumb in poker is that your bets should be proportionate to the size of the pot. Too small, and you allow opponents easy calls. Too big, and you risk losing more than necessary. Balance is key. For instance, preflop and flop bet sizings usually range from 50% to 100% of the pot size. This gives it a reasonable dimension, neither too intimidating nor too inviting.

That said, the value doesn't remain constant and varies according to your position, stack size, and table dynamics. A table of tight players invites more aggressive betting compared to a table filled with loose, aggressive players where more caution is warranted. The position at the table directly influences your bet size. Late positions open the door for higher bets than early positions. Similarly, a shorter stack prompts more caution than a towering stack.

10.2. Betting Lines And Strategy

Betting lines refer to the path you choose in a betting round. In poker, it's not about playing a single hand; it's about plotting a trajectory for the entire game. Every bet you place is a part of a larger strategy, an integral stitch in the canvas of your game plan.

The most common betting lines are value betting and bluffing.

Value betting is implemented when you believe you have the best hand and want to get called by a worse one. An important part of this strategy is to subtly size your bets to extract maximum value. Betting too much might deter weaker hands, whereas betting too little might fail to extract value.

Bluffing, on the other hand, is where the spectacle of poker lies. A bluff is a bet or a series of bets made with a weak hand to make opponents believe you have a strong one. However, reckless or predictable bluffing can lead to serious losses. It's a tool that can either hammer in your victory or nail your defeat.

Semi-bluffing is a variant where you might not have the best hand currently but have a decent chance of drawing into a strong hand. It's a delicate blend of hope and deception.

10.3. The Role of Pot Odds in Betting

Pot odds are a critical element to consider when deciding whether to call a bet. They are the ratio between the current size of the pot and your potential calling cost. In simpler terms, pot odds determine if a call can be profitable in the long run.

Understanding pot odds, however, is only the tip of the iceberg. Calculating the 'outs' (cards that can potentially improve your hand to a winning one) and 'implied odds' (future betting actions in the game) are indispensable skills to successful betting.

10.4. Risk Management in Betting

Risk management and betting go hand in hand. The ability to balance between boldness and caution is paramount. Remember, it's okay to back out and fold your hand if the bet escalates beyond a comfortable risk level. Poker isn't about winning every hand but about strategically winning the right ones.

Preserving your chip stack for more profitable opportunities is a winning strategy in itself. Also, keep your opponents guessing by altering bet sizes and frequencies, hence avoiding predictability.

10.5. Betting Tells

In the world of poker, information is wealth. 'Tells' are physical or behavioural cues from your opponents that might reveal useful information about their hands.

While 'tells' are more prevalent in live games, digital platforms are not devoid of them. Speedy or delayed reactions, quick-checking, or changes in a player's usual betting pattern all might hint at their gameplay.

And with these pieces of information, you can adjust your betting strategy to increase your chances of hogging that coveted pot.

As you navigate the betting landscape, remember what poker legend Doyle Brunson once said, "Poker is a war. People pretend it is a game." And betting is your battlefield. Learn it well, soldier it better, and may the odds ever be in your favour.

Chapter 11. A Champion's Mindset: Psychological Insights for Winning Big

The battle of minds at a poker table is every bit as remarkable as physical combat. It's a field laden with uncertainty, and at its very core, poker is a game inspired by human psychology. Mastering the strategies of the game without understanding the psychology that runs it is akin to trying to win a race without fortifying your stamina. The purpose of this segment is to wander into the mind of a champion poker player, unravel the strands of mindset that set them apart, and equip you with the insights you require to sculpt your mind for optimum performance.

11.1. The Architecture of a Champion's Mind

The fashioning of a winner's mind is an art as much as it is a science. It is a studied construction of cognitive patterns, discipline, focus, and an open mind. When it comes to poker, every well-made decision brings you one inch closer to victory.

1. Discipline: A champion's journey is replete with moments of extraordinary discipline. It is the underlying stone that upholds all other mental attributes. It is discipline that urges a player to fold a losing hand, no matter how promising it initially seemed. Discipline prevents a player from acting impulsively, conscious perseverance in the face of immediate gratification. It favors the ability to follow strategies regardless of emotional dynamisms in the game.

2. Attitude: A mindset that celebrates process over reward, learning

over winning, will always have an edge. This fosters a healthier approach, helping you keep your cool when faced with potential losses or downswings. Attitude harnesses the power to turn setbacks into setups, deepening your understanding of the game over time.

3. Focus: Concentration constitutes a critical part of a champion's mind. It is the ability to zoom in and filter out distractions, paying attention to the smallest details and array of information available at a poker table. From the countenance of your opponents to the patterns of bets, the ability to decode these cues is what sets apart the masters.

4. Open-Mindedness: The mark of an expert is his willingness to remain a perpetual student. The game of poker is continually evolving, and the ability to adapt to its changing dynamics equips you with a strong competitive advantage. Embrace the new and the unexpected, making room for growth and learning.

11.2. Fear and Fearlessness

Fear, in poker, can be a monstrous mind-killer. Being fearful of losing a large pot can prompt poor decisions, making you too risk-averse or too cautious. However, the opposite - fearlessness - can also drive recklessness, leading to excessive risks and imprudent moves.

Champions ride the delicate balance between fear and fearlessness. They maintain control over emotions, making informed and calculated choices. They utilize fear as a compass that guides them away from prospective perilous paths, while using fearlessness to drive timely aggressive actions.

11.3. Emotive Intelligence

Mastering one's psychology also encompasses having an acute understanding of others' emotions at the poker table. This skill, often recognized as emotional intelligence, involves recognizing and interpreting your opponents' behaviors, responses, and possibly, their cards.

1. Observation: Champions are acute observers, studying every small detail about their opponent's behavior. How someone bets, reacts to certain hands, or changes their strategy can peek into their mindset.

2. Empathy: Trying to understand and resonate with an opponent's feeling enhances your ability to predict their moves. By placing yourself in their shoes, you're more likely to read their game better.

11.4. Resilience and Mental Toughness

Poker is an emotional roller-coaster. Experiencing wins might elevate you to cloud nine, but losses could equally drop you down in the dumps. Maintaining an even keel through these highs and lows is paramount. The ability to face defeat but not get defeated, to rise from every fall, to stay positive and motivated, is the robust mental armor champions wear. It's this hard shell of resilience that keeps them going through the toughest games.

11.5. Meditation and Mindfulness

A frequently undervalued tool in the poker world, mindfulness exercises, and meditative practices can help fine-tune your focus, manage stress, and improve your emotional awareness. Not only does it help in handling the anxiety and tension during the game, but it also teaches you to stay present, assuring you don't get caught in the labyrinth of past hands or future predictions.

In conclusion, what transpires within the confines of our craniums is a significant contributor to the outcome at the felt. Poker is an intense mind game and mastering the mental dynamics can give you a deserving edge. It may not guarantee you a win every time, but it assures you're always geared up for the battle. With these psychological insights and tools, you're now equipped to take your poker game to the next level. Success, after all, is largely a matter of hanging on when others have let go.